AN INTERMEDIATE PER
COMPANION FOR POP STUDIES 3

THE WUNDERKEYS ESSENTIAL PIANO COLLECTION

An Intermediate Performance Companion For Pop Studies 3 by Andrea and Trevor Dow
Copyright © 2021 Teach Music Today Learning Solutions
www.teachpianotoday.com and www.wunderkeys.com

WunderKeys® is a registered trademark of Andrea and Trevor Dow
(Teach Music Today Learning Solutions) in the U.S.A. and Canada

TABLE OF CONTENTS

In this book, WunderKeys' greatest intermediate hits have been reworked to create a leveled repertoire collection for use alongside **WunderKeys Intermediate Pop Studies For Piano 3**.

4

THE PACHELBEL SESSION
Inspired by Pachelbel's Canon

7

DEVLIN'S THEME
from The Guardians Of Arranmore

10

ELISE
from The Beethoven Sessions (Inspired by Für Elise)

13

THE RONDO SESSION
from The Amadeus Anthems (Inspired by Rondo Alla Turca)

16

THE WARSAW SESSION
from The Victress Sessions (Inspired by Nocturne In Bb Major)

20

SWORDS OF SHANNON
from The Guardians Of Castlemore (Devlin's Return)

TABLE OF CONTENTS

23
THE MUSETTE SESSION
from The Sebastian Sessions (Inspired by Musette In D Major)

26
THE MOONLIGHT SESSION
from The Beethoven Sessions (Inspired by Moonlight Sonata, Op. 27, No. 2)

30
BETTER DAYS
Original Composition For This Publication

34
THE FIFTH SESSION
from The Beethoven Sessions (Inspired by Symphony No. 5, Op. 67)

38
THE BEACH SESSION
from The Victress Sessions (Inspired by Romance For Violin And Piano, Op. 23)

41
OPEN SPACES
from The Silver Screen Playbook

44
AISLING RISING
from The Guardians Of Ballinmore

47
FÁELÁN'S THEME
from The Guardians Of Arranmore

THE PACHELBEL SESSION
AN E FLAT MAJOR SOLO BY ANDREA DOW

THE PACHELBEL SESSION

DEVLIN'S THEME
A C MINOR SOLO BY ANDREA DOW

DEVLIN'S THEME

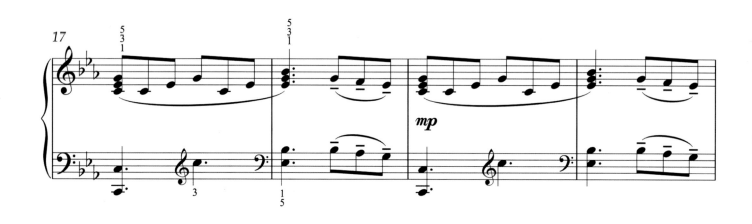

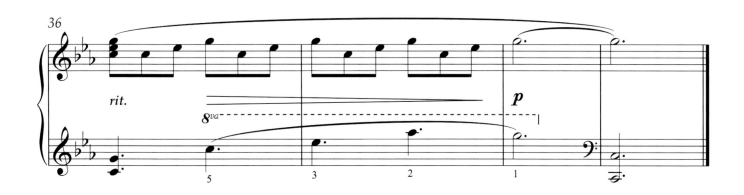

ELISE
AN E MAJOR SOLO BY ANDREA DOW

ELISE

THE RONDO SESSION
A C SHARP MINOR SOLO BY ANDREA DOW

Lively ♩ = 120

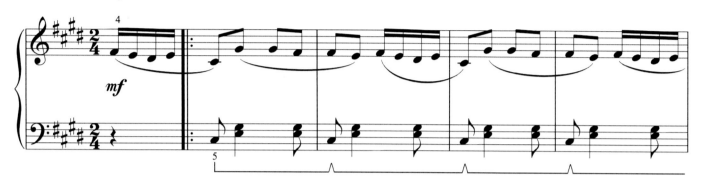

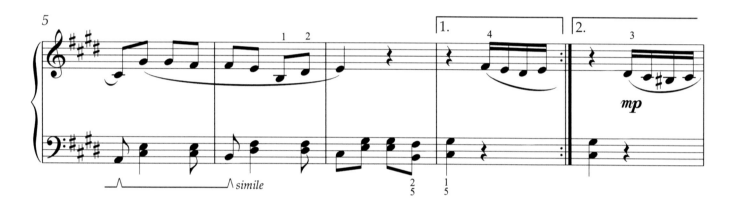

THE RONDO SESSION

THE WARSAW SESSION
AN A FLAT MAJOR SOLO BY ANDREA DOW

Flowing ♩. = 66

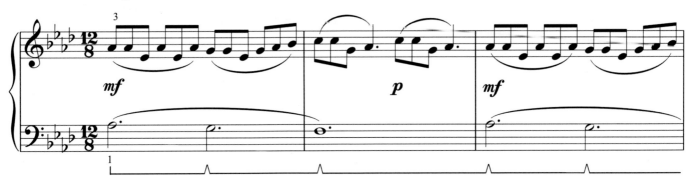

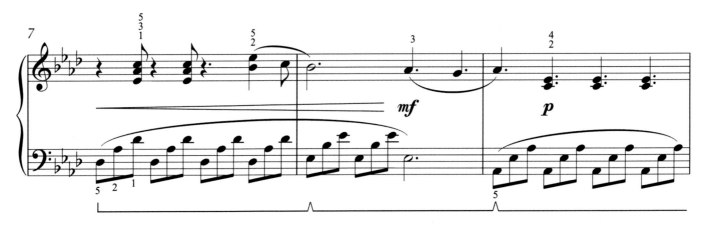

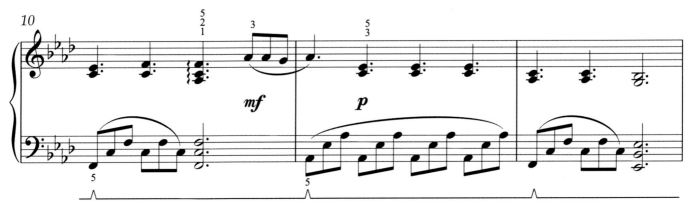

THE WARSAW SESSION

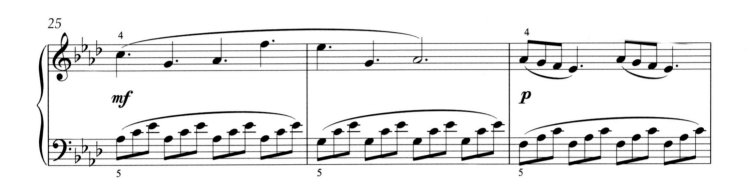

SWORDS OF SHANNON
AN F MINOR SOLO BY ANDREA DOW

With Expression ♩ = 100

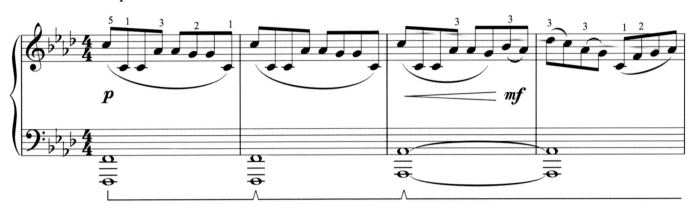

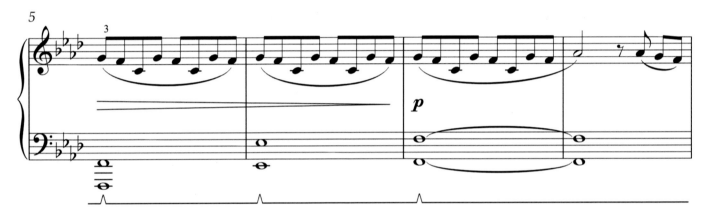

SWORDS OF SHANNON

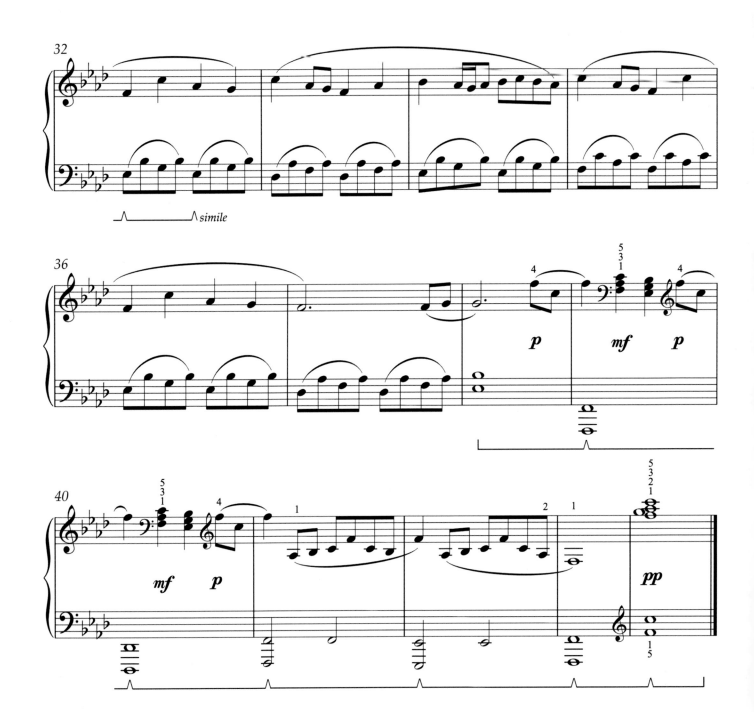

THE MUSETTE SESSION
AN E FLAT MAJOR SOLO BY ANDREA DOW

THE MOONLIGHT SESSION
A C MINOR SOLO BY ANDREA DOW

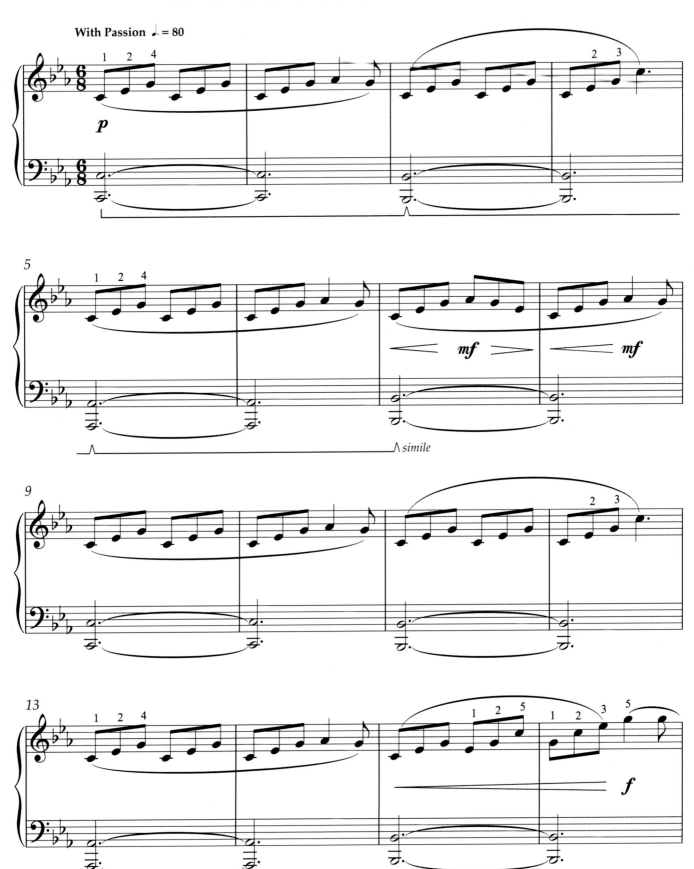

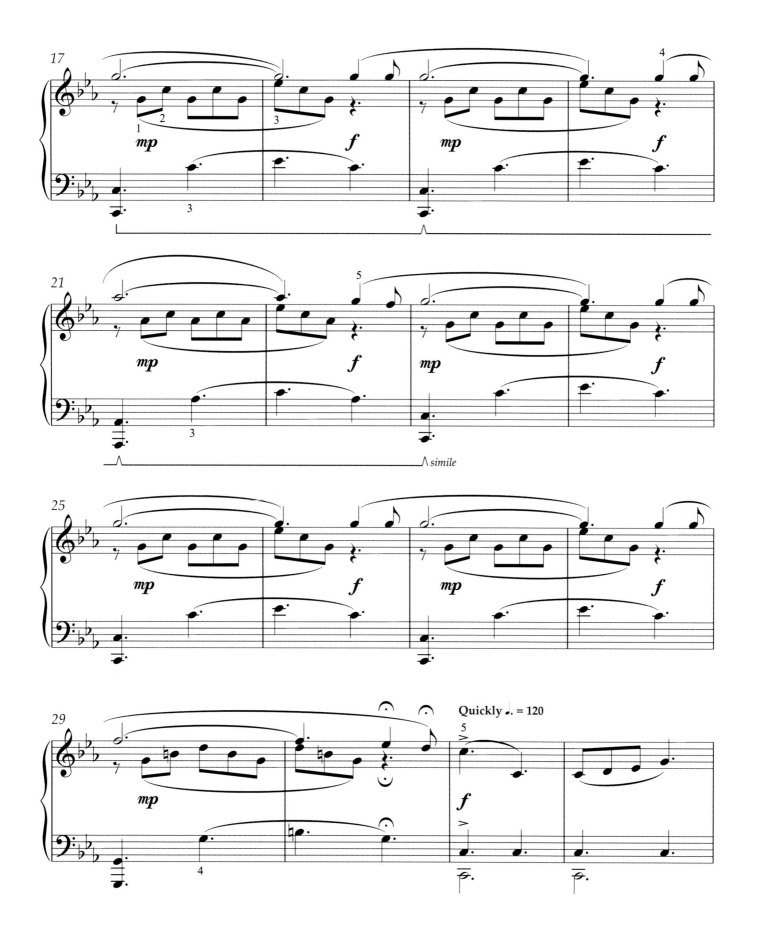

BETTER DAYS
AN E MAJOR SOLO BY ANDREA DOW

BETTER DAYS

BETTER DAYS

BETTER DAYS

THE FIFTH SESSION
A C SHARP MINOR SOLO BY ANDREA DOW

Dramatically ♩ = 126

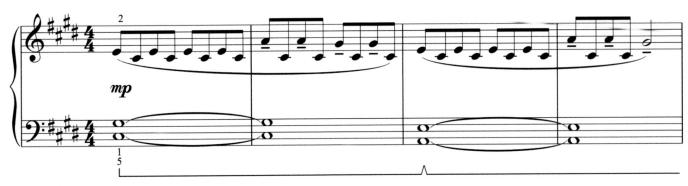

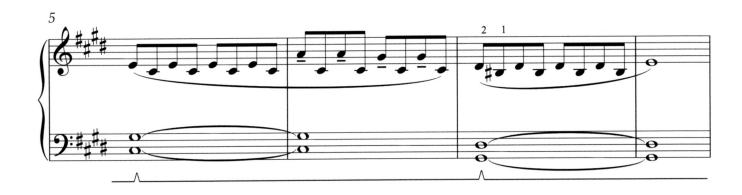

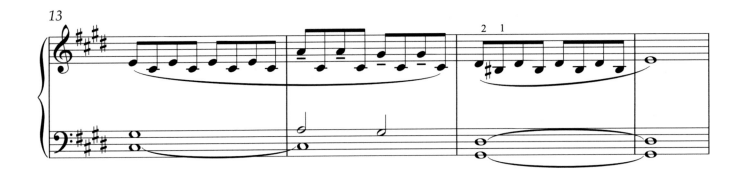

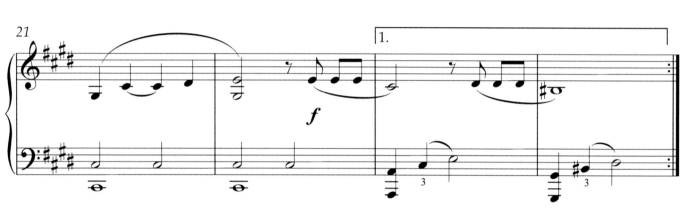

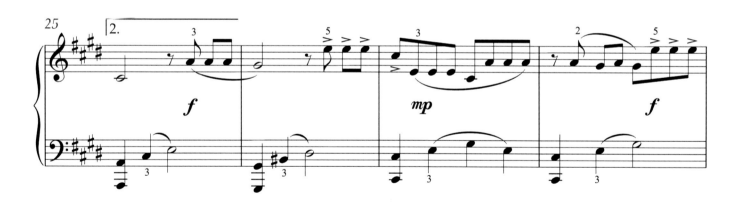

THE FIFTH SESSION

THE BEACH SESSION
AN A FLAT MAJOR SOLO BY ANDREA DOW

THE BEACH SESSION

OPEN SPACES
AN F MINOR SOLO BY ANDREA DOW

Gracefully ♩ = 80

OPEN SPACES

AISLING RISING
AN F MINOR SOLO BY ANDREA DOW

Flowing ♩ = 120

AISLING RISING

FÁELÁN'S THEME
A C SHARP MINOR SOLO BY ANDREA DOW

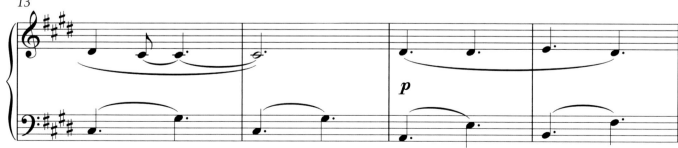

FÁELÁN'S THEME

Made in United States
Orlando, FL
24 September 2024

51918191R10029